THE HISTORICAL METHOD
IN SOCIAL SCIENCE

THE HISTORICAL METHOD
IN SOCIAL SCIENCE

An Inaugural Lecture

by

M. M. POSTAN

*Professor of Economic History in the
University of Cambridge*

CAMBRIDGE
AT THE UNIVERSITY PRESS
1939

CAMBRIDGE
UNIVERSITY PRESS

University Printing House, Cambridge CB2 8BS, United Kingdom

Published in the United States of America by Cambridge University Press, New York

Cambridge University Press is part of the University of Cambridge.

It furthers the University's mission by disseminating knowledge in the pursuit of education, learning and research at the highest international levels of excellence.

www.cambridge.org
Information on this title: www.cambridge.org/9781107635593

© Cambridge University Press 1939

First published 1939
Re-issued 2014

A catalogue record for this publication is available from the British Library

ISBN 978-1-107-63559-3 Paperback

THE HISTORICAL METHOD IN SOCIAL SCIENCE

Few other branches of university study are more indigenous to Cambridge than the one which I have the great honour to represent. It was in Cambridge that Archdeacon Cunningham laid the foundations of economic history as a university subject, and it was out of this University that the long stream of his pioneer books issued. Cunningham was a great missionary, for economic history was to him part of his political and philosophical faith. He believed that English thought, and English politics of his time, wanted rescuing from the a-moral and a-national prejudices of liberal economics and whig history; and it was from economic history as then taught in Germany that the cure would come. This belief led him to concentrate very largely on the problems of economic policy to the exclusion of many of the topics which form the scope of economic history now. Yet it is remarkable how, in spite of his preoccupations, the work has survived the faith which prompted it and in its main outlines endures to our own day. If economic historians of the next generation were able to devote themselves to specialized study, it was because the field was occupied for them and the foundation laid by Cunningham.

But what the generation which followed owed to the man who laid the foundation, the present generation owes to the man who built on them: the first holder of the Chair, the master mason who has preceded me. On the ground on which Dr Clapham has worked and still works he found a mass of half-knowledge, overgrown with pictu-resque and stubborn weeds. This ground he has not only cleared, but in his own in-imitable, lapidary way, has covered with a structure of facts as hard and certain as granite. On his ground and in his manner nothing else remains to be done: so in

Cambridge where the first phase of economic history was begun, the second has just been concluded.

I

With these achievements to precede him, no present holder of the Chair can claim to be a pioneer. He will never know the joy of staking out the first claims and of turning the first sod, or the greatest of all joys, that of inventing new names. Yet he will be a hypocrite if he pretends not to relish the advantages of his position as an inheritor; above all, the great advantage of being able not to engage in his inaugural lecture in the great controversy of history as science *versus* history as art.

In so far as science means accuracy, and art good writing, their respective claims on historians have now been settled, for we all now agree with the Regius Professor that history should be both accurate and readable. But even if both science and art are defined by their objects—science as a search for general causes, art as an exercise in imaginative creation—the issue does not present itself to economic history, though it may still concern other branches of history. For in economic history the practices of its founders, the accident of its rise and the nature of its material, deprive the historian of real choice and condemn him to dwell with the social sciences.

The facts of economic history cannot be shaped, as a personal biography or a field of battle can, into an image with a direct appeal to our artistic sensibilities. Its most effective instrument, as Dr Clapham has so well argued and proved, is the impersonal language of statistical measurements. It came into existence not as an attempt to rival the novel or the drama in the re-creation of life, but as an endeavour to assist in the solution of social problems. Its founders abroad were lawyer-sociologists of the romantic period, Möser, Guizot, Lamprecht, or the economists of the mid-century, Knies, Roscher, List. Its source

8

of inspiration in this country is Adam Smith, and its ethos derives more from Bacon than from Shakespeare. So, much as economic historians would like to rank with the richest and oldest of the arts, they are compelled to serve the poorest and the youngest of sciences.

But for one controversy they have escaped they have raised legions of others. Having gone to dwell with the social sciences they have still to decide the details of the dwelling: what it is to be—detached or semi-detached, and where—in the public halls or the servants' quarters. All these are problems of cohabitation within the social sciences, and the very fact that the sites have not yet been completely marked out makes the choice uncertain and difficult.

Regarded superficially, the mood now prevailing among history's nearest neighbours is very propitious to economic and social history. A new wave of empiricism appears to be sweeping across regions hitherto inhabited by pure theory. The most general, and the least defined of social studies, sociology, is rapidly winding up its interest in comprehensive formulae and is turning into a comparative study of institutions: family, property, legal custom, class division. When done expertly, it merges into the specialized study of social evidence; and since all social evidence, where it is not anthropological or statistical, is bound to be historical, much of sociology has been assuming the character of generalized and universalized history. Similarly, what now passes for political science is in large part concerned with political institutions as they are revealed in recent historical experience. And finally, economics—the field in which economic historians most frequently camp—has entered into one of its empirical phases.

The economists, like the theoretical sociologists of old, only more so, tried to solve the largest possible problems from the least possible knowledge. The ingenuity which went, and still goes, into some of the syllogistic exercises of theoretical economics is only rivalled by the unreality of some of its conclusions. But if some of its conclusions are capable of illuminating real problems of economic life, and economics as a whole is something more than a soufflé of whipped postulates, it is because even the most theoretical of economists sometimes manage to mix their theorems with a little social observation. The fact that the Cambridge economists, from Marshall to Keynes, have always tried to draw upon their personal observations of reality may account for the practical importance of their theoretical constructions. Marshall's capacity for interpolating a new empirical condition at each successive stage of his argument, and of calling in new facts to redress old conclusions, is perhaps the most striking feature of his method. And no reader of Keynes's general theory will fail to observe the central position occupied in it by two acutely observed empirical scales.

But what in books of Marshall or Keynes

is an occasional spark of private wisdom now promises, or shall I say threatens, to become an organized branch of economic study. The realization that their subject has been purer than it ought to be has led the economists to insist upon the need for inductive study. In this country very recently, in the United States and Germany for quite a long time, an ever-growing amount of academic effort has been turned to the collection of economic facts. Studies of individual industries, of individual firms, of price and wage movements, commercial treaties and legislative methods, have been flooding the market. Measured by bulk, most American economic study is devoted to collection of facts. Similarly measured, the syllabus of the Economics Tripos in Cambridge consists very largely of courses on this or that industry, this or that region. And to listen to fashionable economic talk, one might think that the whole race of economists has become converted to the religion of the counting machine.

II

So, superficially, it would appear that history, as the repository of the empirical facts which the economist and sociologist can employ, has come to its own again, and that the social sciences are once again becoming historical. And yet, if truth be known, much of the recent hankering for facts and wooing of facts and amassing of facts, appears to an economic historian as far removed from history and as irrelevant to the real business of empirical study as are the arm-chair fantasies of the sociologists or the pure abstractions of the mathematical economists. For though in a sense all facts are historical facts, and all historical facts are social evidence, the data which the economists and sociologists now accumulate are seldom employed in a way which an economic historian would recognize as historical.

History is something which is both more and less than what sociologists and economists now make of it. It is certainly something more than an assemblage of data. We all know that what now distinguishes the honourable occupation of antiquaries from the questionable occupation of historians is that whereas antiquaries collect facts historians study problems. To a true antiquary all past facts are welcome, to an historian facts are of little value unless they are causes, or parts of causes, or the causes of causes, of the phenomena which he studies. A description of an industry wherein all the facts which strike the student's eye are assembled is a piece of economic antiquarianism. Economic history ends at the point at which the facts cease to answer questions, and the nearer the questions are to social problems and the more completely the problems dominate the search for facts, the nearer is the study to the true function of history in social science.

These obvious remarks may strike economists as an admonition delivered at a wrong address, for in the past the economists were apt to justify their indifference to historical study by the alleged irrelevance of economic history to the problems of economics. With this accusation we shall presently deal: for the alleged irrelevance of the topics of economic history is not altogether the historian's fault. But even if it were, the fact remains that the amount of useful knowledge or just ordinary sense that can be derived from the flood of empirical studies is incommensurate with the effort expended on them. And if that is so, it is not because the searchers are incompetent, the evidence intractable, or other sciences uncooperative, but because the main direction of the so-called empirical economics is at fault. The economists so seldom derive from their facts the theoretical knowledge they require because they do not ask from their facts the kind of question facts can answer.

We have just said that the nearer the question is to a social problem, the more completely it dominates a fact, so much the nearer it is to history and to the true business of social science. This economists understand only too well; what they perhaps do not realize is that for the purposes of empirical study the question, the dominating problem, is not necessarily given by the theoretical conclusions of abstract economics. The prevailing tendency among economists is to believe that, having arrived at a conclusion by a long and complicated series of deductions from original propositions, they can then proceed to verify it on historical and statistical facts. I do not want to suggest that that verification is always impossible, or where possible undesirable. In fields in which the original assumptions correspond closely to an experience which is real, easily discoverable, and limited in range, conclusions are sometimes arrived at, which subsequent empirical study can check. No reader of Taussig's book on the History of American Tariffs, or Viner's on Canada's Foreign Trade, or Bresciani-Turoni's on German Inflation, can fail to notice how well some propositions of economics can be supported by historical facts. Far be it from me to deny the possibility or the value of attempts at verification such as these. But the bulk of the empirical studies do not verify any of the conclusions of economic theory, for the simple reason that most of the conclusions are so derived as to be incapable of empirical verification, and some of them are so constructed as not to require it and to be illuminating and important even though unverifiable.

Economists have lately been only too anxious to abandon the logical position which they have so proudly occupied since the days of Ricardo, Mill, Menger, and the older Keynes. The methodological assumption and justification of theoretical economics is the belief that it covers a field of problems in which knowledge could best be acquired by the exercise of deductive reasoning. In the modest opinion of an outsider like myself, this assumption has been borne out by the history of economic science. In the fields which economists have chosen as their own, they have reaped a crop of conclusions far greater in bulk and finer in substance than anything they could have obtained by the inductive study of facts. But the price of deduction is abstraction: the logical rigour and consistency of economic propositions is a direct consequence of the fact that the fundamental concepts, the original assumptions and the successive stages of economic argument are all treated in isolation from the rest of social environment. And abstraction accounts for the unhelpfulness of economics as well as for its success. Having been derived by way of continuous and accumulated abstraction, and composed of *a priori* concepts, economic propositions cannot be directly applied to facts for purposes of either policy or verification. Within their limits they are as true as, if not truer than, any other branch of scientific knowledge. Where they are unsatisfactory is not in their being wrong but

18

in their being incomplete. And where the empirical studies can help, is not in making them truer but in making them fuller; not so much in testing their often untestable truth on facts, as in making them more relevant and tangible by supplementing them with scientific thought on those aspects of social life from which they have been abstracted.

This residuum of social life fills the background of economic theories as a kind of invisible presence: mentioned frequently and always reverentially, but seldom studied, never analysed. Sometimes it makes a fleeting entry into an economic theorem in the famous disguise of "other conditions being equal", only to pass out of discussion with its incognito intact. Even though the one thing we know for certain about the "other conditions" is that they cannot possibly be equal, little is done to establish their true identity, to go behind their variety and flux, and to understand the intricacies of their pattern.

Sometimes these other conditions enter economic theory in the form of specific assumptions. Certain modes of social behaviour which are known intimately to affect the economic problem under discussion, but have not been selected for manipulation by economists, are then named, and left named, as special assumptions. So special are they that the whole practical value, the whole significance of the theorem when applied, indeed its very chance of being applied, depends on the knowledge of the modes of behaviour thus assumed. And yet the knowledge is not there, and little attempt is made to obtain it.

Thus in a recent restatement of the theory of international trade,[1] that trade is shown to be primarily "caused by the uneven distribution of the factors" of production, and important conclusions are made to depend on the interregional movements of capital and labour. But what that "uneven

[1] B. Ohlin, *International Trade, passim*, and especially pp. 48 and 58 and ch. xvii.

distribution" was and is—its causes and prospects—is unknown and taken for granted. Similarly assumed and almost equally unknown are the all-important movements of the "factors". For in spite of the interesting illustrations which the author draws from his Scandinavian and American experience, and a statistical sketch of the relations between prices and foreign lending, the social processes behind the migration of capital and labour still remain unexplored and unexplained.

In the same way a generally accepted formulation of the theory of wages contains a set of propositions dependent on a number of assumed social conditions, and among them population, the supply of capital, the people's ability or willingness to work, and technical inventions.[1] The theory establishes clearly that its conclusions as to wages and employment will in each concrete case be dependent on what those social conditions happen to be. But

[1] J. R. Hicks, *A Theory of Wages*, p. 114.

do we know enough about the conditions to be able to give reality to the author's proposition? What social causes, psychological, political, institutional, determined in the past and are likely to go on determining the changing attitudes of labour or the changing supplies of capital or the development of applied science or the outbursts of technical ingenuity?

Or let us take an example more up-to-date and nearer Cambridge. Mr Keynes's famous general theory of employment, if I understand it correctly, makes a set of conclusions about employment, the rate of interest, and in certain contingencies also prices and wages, dependent on two scales of human behaviour: the propensities of men to consume different proportions of their income, and their preferences for the different degrees of liquidity in which savings can be held. The existence of these scales is acutely observed, their importance as concepts has been universally acknowledged, their names now belong to the basic English of economics. But how much do the economists know about them? Do they know or have they explained the complex social process which throughout history has determined the employment of income and its allocation to consumption or rather to consuming classes, or have they tried to discover what social forces lurk behind liquidity preferences?

I could multiply the examples *ad infinitum*, but I hope my meaning is clear without them. Such assumptions about the social background as are made by economists, indeed the very fact that they are made, show that they are regarded as important. The fact that although they are as yet unknown they do not block the activity of the economists shows that they are regarded as capable of being known. Why then is there so little empirical economics dealing not only with the statistical verification of economic propositions, but also with the disclosure and analysis of their social conditions?

I know that by asking this question I am inviting the retort and the advice not to be in a hurry. For what the economists have not yet done they may do yet. But if that is the retort, I should like to be allowed the dismal prophecy that the same causes which prevented the economists from engaging in these problems yesterday will prevent them both to-day and to-morrow. The social topics which they themselves assume, but do not settle, belong to regions of enquiry which are outside, i.e. either beyond or beneath, the typical economist's tastes and powers. They are particles of concrete and tangible reality, their study demands constant reference to the whole combination of social forces, their logical problem is that of multiple interrelation, indeed an interrelation so multiple as to make the work of abstraction impossible and undesirable. My impertinent suggestion therefore is that those fields which the economists are obviously unable or unwilling to cultivate belong to other people.

They are the true regions of empirical study; and had better be left to students who specialize in complex social situations, who search for past causes (and all causes are past causes), and who above all do not expect their result ever to reach the precision of a mathematical formula, and will therefore not be disappointed by the more indeterminate results which can be derived from the study of historical reality. In short, the regions are those of economic history, and by occupying them and working them historians can make the one contribution to economic science which at present nobody else seems to be making.

III

I hope that by thus defining the character of the contribution which empirical study in general, and economic history in particular, can make to economic science, I have not given the impression of extravagance. For what I have just said about the indeterminate results of historical study recalls the statement with which I started: namely, that history is not only more but also less than the use to which it is sometimes turned by social scientists. If economists err on the side of disparagement, by limiting too narrowly the range of historical enquiry, sociologists err on the side of extravagance by exalting unduly the function of historical facts. They expect from them final and instantaneous solutions of all the most profound of society's problems. And they are convinced that if history has so far failed to yield a complete science of society and to found the engineering technique of politics, the fault is not history's but the historian's. There is an assumption throughout the whole of their recent work that in the hands of sociologists historical evidence can easily be made to yield the secrets which it refuses to historians. Hence the embarrassingly ambitious—and to an historian the embarrassingly crude—treatises on society in general, property in general, class in general, which are produced by sociologists on the basis of evidence originally collected by historians. Hence, also, the attempts to wring from historical facts theoretical lessons, lessons which send shivers up the historian's spine for the violence they do to facts, the simplicities they impose upon life.

This aversion of historians to the maltreatment of their facts by sociologists is a result neither of stupidity nor of ignorance, but of experience and disillusionment. The historical method in social science has its own history, and that history is filled with the tombstones of historical schools, which claimed for their method more than it could give. The scientific employment of social, legal and constitutional history began in the attempts of people in the eighteenth and the early nineteenth centuries to derive from history useful political and philosophical lessons. Even the notions of historical relativity and anti-philosophical scepticism which mark the rise of the so-called historical schools of jurisprudence and politics in the early nineteenth century were tinged with the belief that where reason failed historical study might succeed. History, it was thought, could, when suitably employed, not only show up the imperfection of rational propositions but also support general propositions of its own. But the subsequent two or three generations, above all the mid-decades of the Victorian age, taught history yet another lesson. For while the historical school of jurisprudence, Savigny and the rest, found it only too easy to demonstrate the imperfection of the universal principles of rationalist jurisprudence and political theory, they have not been able to replace them with a single historical principle capable of direct general formulation. And similarly while Knies, Roscher and Schmoller found no difficulty in showing the relativity of Adam Smith's and Ricardo's ideas, and their dependence upon circumstances which were purely

English and purely temporary, they were unable to derive from history anything in the nature of alternative principles capable of replacing the ones they had rejected.

So now at last the practitioners of the historical method have discovered, what its founders may not have realized, that even though historians and theoreticians travel on the same road, they not only use different vehicles, but also reach different destinations. For the destination of the theoretical sociologists—general universal laws, directly derived from empirical evidence and explicitly stated in generic terms—are things beyond the reach of the most flighty and peregrinatory of historians.

Why this is so all historians and many non-historians now realize. As I have already said, the degree of generalization which the theoretical economists have achieved in their field, and which some philosophers of law would like jurisprudence to achieve in theirs, has been made possible only at the price of abstraction.

Now, history also can and also does abstract to some extent; but the extent makes all the difference. Abstraction of a sort is an essential condition of all processes of thought; without it we can use no language; the historian abstracts his facts and groups them into classes and types merely by using words. By calling the war of 1815 a "war", and the war of 1914 a "war", and the Punic War a "war", the historian creates generic terms and abstracts up to a certain degree. But the degree, the length to which he is prepared to go on abstracting, is of vital importance. Beyond a certain point abstraction robs the fact of all historical reality. What gives facts of history, or all social facts, their worth as evidence, and their value for causal analysis, is their existence, their tangible and verifiable reality. Only tangible and concrete phenomena can be fitted into a social setting and demonstrated as a link in a chain of causation. But when abstraction has gone so far as entirely to separate the fact from its social environment, when the concept of war is so employed as to exclude all the historical circumstances of the war of 1815 and of that of 1914 and of the Punic War, the facts of history cease to be facts, lose their value as evidence, and the justification of history as a search for concrete causes goes.

The topics of history, however general in some of their aspects, have an individual existence, and it is for that reason that the historian, however generalizing he is by temperament and however sociological in interests, always writes biographies, accounts of single combinations of circumstances. The historian's work is biographical, even when the subject of the biography is such an impersonal and sociological phenomenon as my own subject of study at the moment: rural society in the Middle Ages. Where the historian shows his scientific preoccupations, and qualifies for membership of the social sciences, is in concentrating the study of his individual subject on its relevance to general and theoretical problems. He studies rural society in the Middle Ages, which is a unique and unrepeatable phenomenon, because the study is relevant to such sociological problems as the correlation of population, social structure, social class and tenure, economic technique and legal concepts. But unlike a sociologist he refuses to ask universal questions or try to formulate general laws.

Confronted with the same problems a sociologist would write a book on the connection between social structure and economic technique in all places and all centuries, as exhibited by historical evidence of every country and every age; he would write a similar book on all family, all class, all property. But to an historian these frontal attacks on theoretical problems, even when delivered with massed battalions of historical facts, are not history; and in my opinion they are not even social science. Social study in its empirical ranges deals with entire social patterns; however abstracted and however simplified, its facts are still too complex for a single and a simple prediction. And at the cost of yet another repetition, we must insist that the penalty of being sufficiently concrete to be real is the impossibility of being sufficiently abstract to be exact. And laws which are not exact, predictions which are not certain, generalizations which are not general, are truer when shown in a concrete instance or in one of their unique manifestations than they are when expressed in quasi-universal terms.

The only thing therefore which economic and social history can do for social science is to go on studying individual situations, rural society in thirteenth-century England, the rise of modern industry in the eighteenth-century midlands, labour's attitudes to wages and hours in the first half of the nineteenth century, technical education in Germany in the second half of the nineteenth century, the English wool-trade in the Middle Ages, etc., etc. But while studying social situations it must ask questions and look for answers capable of revealing the action of social causes. In studying rural society in the thirteenth century one may demonstrate the economic transformation produced by the growth of population, and in studying the labour attitude to wages one may lay bare the social forces which once converted a portion of humanity into a capitalist factor of production and still go on affecting its mobility and economic tractability. In studying technical education in Germany and the relation of factories to universities one may reveal the causes which are capable of stimulating an independent movement of technical progress. These microscopic problems of historical research can and should be made microcosmic—capable of reflecting worlds larger than themselves. It is in this reflected flicker of truth, the revelations of the general in the particular, that the contribution of the historical method to social science will be found.

34

IV

Is a light so meagre worth shedding? Is it worth giving implied answers, incapable of being put into words, to assumed questions which do not suffer being asked? Is not the whole enterprise of social and economic history as part of social science a mere attempt to overcome the difficulty of scientific thought by shirking it?

These doubts are not for me to answer. Had my subject to-day been "The Value of Historical Study" I should have taken refuge in the common truth that historical knowledge has a virtue which, like that of all knowledge, is independent of its value as science. But as my subject is not the virtue of history but its scientific use, I can only plead in defence the common limitations and common hopes of all social sciences. The value of the historical contribution to the science of humanity is essentially the same as that of all the other contributions: small and uncertain. Whether it is hopeful, as well as being small and in spite of being uncertain, depends on the prospect of the social sciences as a whole, and not on that of history alone. For the uncertainty of historical results is due not to their being produced by historians, but to their being based on social facts. The real question is therefore not whether it is worth the social scientist's while to take the economic historian in as a partner, but whether it is worth his while to set up in business at all. And if I personally am hopeful about the contribution of history, it is because I am not hopeless about the task of social science.

The reason why I am not hopeless is perhaps due to the fact that I am not over-ambitious. I do not believe that the science of society will ever achieve the perfection of astronomy, but neither do I think that scientific thought is impossible or useless on lower ranges of perfection. The perfect achievement of scientific endeavour is to produce in man that certainty of expecta-tion on which action can be based. This absolute certainty is the very opposite of the infinity of possibilities which every situation presents to a savage or a child. Between the perfect astronomical anticipation of the eclipse and the ignorance of a child as to what will follow a rapid movement of hand, a temporary disappearance of the mother, there are infinite variations and degrees in the certainty of anticipation. The path of science is that of progressive reduction in the choice of expectation, and the further the choice is reduced the nearer is thought to the ideal of science and the further it is from primitive ignorance.

Few branches of science, even astronomy, can claim to have reduced all the alternative expectations to one; on the other hand I cannot imagine social studies in combination as incapable of achieving any reduction at all. No matter how much we study wars we shall perhaps never be able to formulate a single generic law as to the cause of war; similarly, no matter how much we study rural society we shall never be able to express the interdependence of population and agricultural technique in a mathematical formula. But, as long as each concrete instance is studied with relevance to real problems, the accumulated results—that is to say, the accumulated analysis of the causes at work—does, and will still more in the future, create a knowledge of society which stands in the same relation to the savage ignorance now prevailing as life's experience or life's wisdom, with its limited range of expectations, stands to the unlimited range of an infant. That position of collective wisdom or historical experience will not be a complete and a perfect science, but for that matter so few of the sciences are. We are hopeful because we are modest; we are modest because we are historians: because the experience of a century of historiography has made us wiser than we should have been a hundred years ago as to what history can and cannot do. Our science, like charity, begins at home.